THE GADIANTON ROBBERS

To Talena and Jay Dee Kerr, with much love

Sherrie Johnson

To Lele and Carson, with much love

Tyler Lybbert

Hi, I'm Havvah! We're Nephites, so we know all about the Book of Mormon.

Watch for me, Leah, and my brother and sister on the pages of this book.

I'll tell you anything you need to know. The first important thing is that I'm Helam.

Printed in Mexico.

10 9 8 7 6 5 4 3 2

ISBN 0-87579-769-5

Designed by Craig Geertsen.

THE GADIANTON ROBBERS

WRITTEN BY
SHERRIE JOHNSON

ILLUSTRATED BY
TYLER LYBBERT

You can read this story yourself in 3 Nephi, chapters 3 and 4.

DESERET BOOK COMPANY
SALT LAKE CITY, UTAH

Lachoneus was astonished as he read the letter from Giddianhi. The letter demanded that Lachoneus and his people join the wicked band of Gadianton robbers. If they did not, the robbers said they would destroy the people. But Lachoneus was a righteous man who could not be frightened by robbers.

The robbers are the bad guys!

Gid-ee-AN-hi is the leader of a band called the Gadianton robbers.

You say it, Lah-CONE-ee-us. He's the governor of the Nephites.

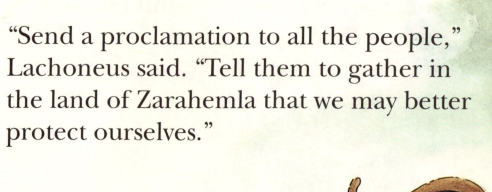

"Send a proclamation to all the people," Lachoneus said. "Tell them to gather in the land of Zarahemla that we may better protect ourselves."

A proclamation is an order telling people what to do.

The people obeyed. By the thousands and by the tens of thousands, they came. As Lachoneus instructed, they brought their horses, chariots, cattle, flocks, grain, and food so that they would have enough supplies to last for seven years.

Lachoneus also built a strong wall around the city of Zarahemla. He organized the armies of the Nephites and the Lamanites and chose chief captains. Gidgiddoni, a great prophet among the people, was chosen chief captain over all the other captains. After the armies were organized, Lachoneus ordered them to stand guard around the wall.

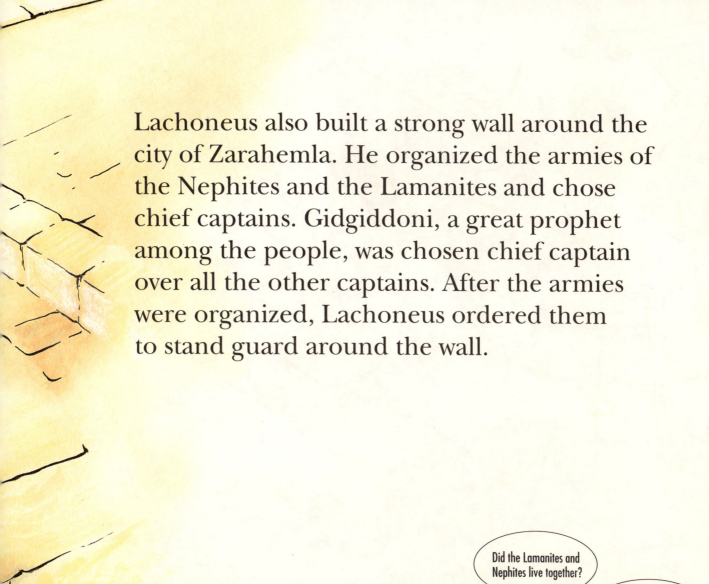

Did the Lamanites and Nephites live together?

At this time, there were Lamanites who believed in God, and they lived with the Nephites.

His name is fun to say. It's Gid-gid-DOE-ni.

The people of the land set to work making weapons, armor, shields, and bucklers. But they needed to do more than prepare food and weapons. Lachoneus warned his people, "Except ye repent of all your sins and pray unto the Lord, you will not be delivered from the hands of those Gadianton robbers."

So great and marvelous were the prophecies of Lachoneus that great fear came upon the people. They knew the words were true, and they began to repent of their sins. They fasted and prayed that God would deliver them from the Gadianton robbers.

But preparing for war made the people impatient. They begged Gidgiddoni, "Let us fall upon these robbers and destroy them before they destroy us."

Gidgiddoni answered, "The Lord forbids it. If we go against them, the Lord will not be with us. We will wait until they come against us. Then the Lord will deliver the robbers into our hands."

Besides being strong, Gidgiddoni was wise.

That's what I want to be!

The Gadianton robbers, who had been hiding in the mountains and in the wilderness, took over the lands the people had left. But the valuable possessions were gone, and there was no food. Even the animals were gone. The robbers had nothing to eat. They knew they would soon starve, but they were afraid to farm the land. They thought the people of Zarahemla would war against them while they were farming.

So the Gadianton robbers prepared
to invade the city of Zarahemla.
They shaved their heads. They
painted themselves with blood. They
tied lambskins about their loins. Then
crowning themselves with head plates,
they attacked the people of Zarahemla.

When the people saw the ferocious robbers coming against them, they fell to the earth.

"They're afraid of us!" the Gadianton robbers shouted and rushed forward.

But the people of God were not afraid—they were praying. They arose as the robbers fell upon them, and in the strength of the Lord, they fought with might and courage.

Despite the terrible threats Giddianhi had made in his letter, the people of Zarahemla won the battle. Frightened, the Gadianton robbers fled into the wilderness. The people of Zarahemla followed until Giddianhi was killed. Then they returned to their place of security.

But some of the robbers had escaped, and they did not give up. They regained their strength and chose a new leader named Zemnarihah. He organized the robbers, and once more they marched against the city of Zarahemla. However, the robbers still had no food. Seeing that his men were about to perish from hunger, Zemnarihah ordered them to return to the wilderness.

You say it, Zem-nah-RYE-hah.

Gidgiddoni knew of their plan. He was afraid the robbers would regain their strength and come again to battle. He knew they must be stopped, or the war would go on for years and many people would die. That night he sent out his armies.

When the Gadianton robbers awoke, they were surrounded. Terrified, thousands of them surrendered. Those who would not surrender were killed. Their leader, Zemnarihah, was hanged from a tree, and the tree was cut down as a warning to all robbers. "May all who seek for power and secret combinations fall to the earth even as this man has fallen to the earth!" the people shouted as the tree fell to the ground.

What are secret combinations?

That's when people plot together to carry out their own evil plans instead of doing God's will.

Then singing and weeping for joy, the people of Zarahemla cried, "Blessed be the name of the Lord God Almighty!" For they knew that it was God who had delivered them from the hands of their enemies.